594.56   Cerullo, Mary M.
CER
          The octopus.

$16.99   13BT01545

DATE			

The
Octopus
Phantom of the Sea

The
Octopus
Phantom of the Sea

Text by
Mary M. Cerullo

Photographs by
Jeffrey L. Rotman

COBBLEHILL BOOKS
Dutton New York

To Professors James D. Hume and Chester A. Roys,
who taught their students by example that
science is a lifelong adventure. —MMC

To Isabelle Delafosse, a great octopus diver. —JLR

ACKNOWLEDGMENTS

Many thanks to James Cosgrove of the Royal British Columbia Museum, Victoria, British Columbia, and Dr. Clyde F. E. Roper of the Department of Invertebrate Zoology, National Museum of Natural History, Smithsonian Institution, Washington, D.C., for the time and careful attention they lavished on the manuscript. Their firsthand knowledge of cephalopods helped me sort out conflicting facts. Any mistakes are from my interpretation of the facts. —MMC

Drawing on page 17 is by C. Michael Lewis
Photograph on page 39 copyright © by Jim Cosgrove
Photograph on page 51 copyright © by Paul Humann

Library of Congress Cataloging-in-Publication Data
Cerullo, Mary M.
The octopus : phantom of the sea / text by Mary M. Cerullo ;
photographs by Jeffrey L. Rotman.
p.   cm.
Includes bibliographical references and index.
Summary: Describes the physical characteristics, feeding and mating habits, and defense mechanisms of octopuses, and gives information about other cephalopods, including the squid, the cuttlefish, and the chambered nautilus.
ISBN 0-525-65199-3
1. Octopus—Juvenile literature. [1. Octopus.]
I. Rotman, Jeffrey L., ill. II. Title.
QL430.3.02C47   1996   594'.56—dc20   96-13971   CIP   AC

Published in the United States by Cobblehill Books,
an affiliate of Dutton Children's Books,
a division of Penguin Books USA Inc.,
375 Hudson Street, New York, New York 10014
Designed by Charlotte Staub
Printed in Hong Kong
First Edition   10 9 8 7 6 5 4 3 2 1

Contents

*The giant octopus can change its color and skin texture to match the background
of an aquarium tank or the ocean floor.*

Chapter One

A Giant Among Octopuses

Curled up inside a dimly lit aquarium tank is one of the world's most magnificent creatures, the giant North Pacific octopus. At this moment, it is plastered against the wall of its tank like a huge wad of chewed bubble gum. A visitor glances into the tank, looks up at the identification label, and protests, "There's no octopus in here!" Even if the spectator spots the coiled creature, he would have a hard time imagining the splendor of this animal in the open sea. If it could stretch out to its full length, this octopus would unfurl a circle of arms fifteen feet across.

After dark, when the crowds have gone, the octopus is alert and restless. It explores every inch of the tank, looking for a means of escape. It finds a small tear in the screen covering of the tank which the aquarium keeper had forgotten to repair. It flicks one arm through the hole. Then, slowly, silently, the octopus oozes sixty pounds of boneless body through the two-inch-wide slit. It slides around behind-the-scenes like animated Jell-O, searching for other aquarium specimens to eat. The next morning, a surprised aquarist finds the fugitive in another tank, nestled among the shells of its former neighbors.

A continent away, a scientist is preparing to visit another giant octopus. Jim Cosgrove, a Canadian researcher with the Royal British Columbia Museum in Victoria, British Columbia, pulls on a rubber dry suit, a scuba outfit designed to keep him warm in the 40° F water. Jim believes that the best way to learn about octopuses is to study them in their own environment, so he has spent thousands of hours in the frigid North Pacific Ocean observing these fascinating *mollusks*, cousins to clams and snails.

Jim and his dive partner tumble into an emerald green sea. The murky water, a thick broth of microscopic plants and animals, makes it difficult to see five feet ahead of them. This just adds to the challenge of finding a sea creature that is nearly invisible even in an aquarium tank. But Jim knows where to hunt for the elusive giant octopus (*Octopus dofleini*) that grows to legendary size here.

On the seafloor 80 feet below the surface, Jim finds a pile of scallop shells next to a boulder cave. As obvious as a street sign, the empty shells mark the entrance to an octopus den. An octopus tosses the shells outside its den after each meal. Jim aims his flashlight inside the cave. Two shiny black eyes reflect the light. The octopus is at home.

Jim sorts through the octopus's garbage heap and makes a note of the number and kinds of shells he finds. Then he clears away the debris. He will return a week later to see what new shells the octopus has discarded. This will help Jim estimate how much the octopus eats in a week, although he knows the octopus doesn't always eat at home. It may have another den at the other end of its range and several "snacking spots" along the way. By picking through the refuse outside many octopus dens, Jim has discovered that each octopus has its own favorite food. One leaves a pile of red rock crab shells. One prefers scallops, another heart cockles, while still another eats only abalone.

Giant octopuses will vary their diet with anything they can grab, including birds and fishes. Several people waiting for a ferry in Washington State saw a giant octopus reach out of the water and yank a sea gull off its perch atop the octopus's rock den. Other octopuses have been observed chasing their prey right onto land.

Unfortunately for the giant octopus, nearly every other animal in the North Pacific loves to eat *it*. Octopus eggs and newborn octopuses are devoured by bottom-dwelling fishes, crabs, and sea stars. Large cod and halibut, as well as sea lions, harbor seals, and porpoises, hunt full-grown octopuses.

Not surprisingly, this octopus views Jim as another potential predator. It retreats deeper into its den. Jim knows it would be useless to try to pull the animal out. Instead, he squirts a mildly irritating chemical into the den—just enough to annoy, but not to harm the animal. Within seconds, a large octopus pops out of the den. When it spies Jim, it turns white with fear. It digs its arms into the sand, prepared for flight. Jim and his dive companion keep their distance. The octopus bobs nervously up and down as it watches them. Gradually, the animal's curiosity gets the better of it. It creeps over to Jim and gently touches his mask with the tip of one arm. It brings up more arms to investigate Jim's dry suit and tank. A rainbow of colors ripples across the octopus's skin.

A giant Pacific octopus gently touches the face mask of marine biologist Jim Cosgrove.

The octopus, its curiosity aroused, moves in for a closer look.

Finally, the octopus releases its grip on the ocean floor and drapes itself around Jim's shoulders. It spins Jim around like an awkward couple on a dance floor. Jim enjoys his encounter with the octopus, knowing that as long as he stays calm, he is not in danger. "An octopus explores and envelops you. It doesn't try to bite. It's actually enjoyable. If I became uncomfortable with the situation, I could make it go away. Anyway, an octopus tires very easily."

After a few minutes, the octopus is exhausted. It releases its partner and turns to jet away. Jim scoops up the tired dancer and stuffs it inside a mesh collecting bag. On the way to the surface, Jim avoids hungry sea lions that would snatch away his prize.

*By capturing, tagging, and releasing octopuses on a regular basis, Jim Cosgrove
has learned that a giant Pacific octopus can gain up to a pound a week
until it tops 100 pounds!*

Back on board the boat, Jim places the octopus in a plastic tub and drains out the water. From a small tag on its body, Jim recognizes this animal as one he had captured the week before. He weighs it, determines its sex, and checks it for scars, wounds, and amputated arms. This 60-pound male gained six pounds in ten days, more than half a pound a day!

Jim releases the octopus near its den and it quickly jets away. By the time this octopus is full-grown, it may weigh 100 pounds or more, while an adult female may reach 60 pounds. *The Guinness Book of World Records* claims the largest giant octopus ever caught, captured in these same waters off western Canada in 1957,

A newly freed octopus jets back to the safety of its den.

7

weighed 600 pounds and was 31 feet across. Jim is skeptical. It's hard to measure an octopus accurately, he cautions, because "they stretch a lot."

Back inside the aquarium, the captive giant octopus sits quietly curling and uncurling one arm, like a child playing with a yo-yo. Its horizontal eyes grow wider as a flock of schoolchildren rushes up to the tank. A shiny necklace catches the octopus's attention. It pulls itself up to the glass window and stares at one of the curious onlookers. For a moment, two pairs of eyes lock together, one human, one mollusk. Each seems to be studying the other. Then the human one blinks and turns away.

Chapter Two

The Nature of the Octopus

The giant octopus may be the best-known octopus because authors and moviemakers have sensationalized its size and supposed danger for so long. French authors Victor Hugo and Jules Verne terrorized their readers with tales of octopuses and giant squids battling men, ships, and submarines. In 1866, Hugo's *Toilers of the Sea* did for octopuses what Peter Benchley's *Jaws* did for sharks a hundred years later: turned them into hunted, hated

Sailors long ago told tales of the kraken, *a sea monster with many arms that could sink a ship. These stories may have been based on sightings of giant octopuses or giant squids.*

sea monsters. Hugo described the octopus as "Supple as leather, tough as steel, cold as night! . . . It draws you to it and into it, and bound, glued, and powerless, you feel yourself slowly absorbed into the frightful sack that is the monster itself."

There are over 150 species of octopuses, yet they rarely attack humans, and then only after being provoked. The octopus has been called hideous, repulsive, and grotesque. Others say it is timid, intelligent, and engaging. What is the *real* octopus like? Is it a devilfish or a misunderstood myth?

Without a doubt, the octopus is a creature of contradictions.

Soft, supple skin conceals a boneless body of surprising strength. Even a three-pound octopus can hold onto a diver with 40 pounds of force; a large octopus exerts 600 pounds of pull. Yet, although it is well-equipped with eight powerful arms, a sharp beak, and poison, an octopus would rather retreat than fight.

This cousin of lowly clams, oysters, and snails is one of the most advanced animals in the sea. The octopus is an animal without a backbone—an *invertebrate*—yet it has a remarkably well-developed nervous system, brain, and eyes. It sees quite well

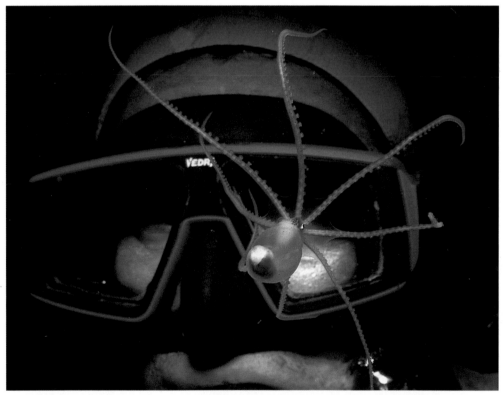

There are over 150 species of octopuses, many of which are the size of this diminutive Red Sea specimen perched on a diver's mask.

The largest octopus in the world, the giant Pacific octopus may reach a length of twenty feet.

underwater. It can solve problems, like figuring out how to open a jar to reach a tasty crab inside. It appears to be able to learn to perform tasks simply by watching other octopuses do them. And it remembers what it learns. Its intelligence is so remarkable that the octopus has been called "the primate of the sea," a flattering comparison to the mental ability of monkeys and apes.

Octopus Anatomy

The octopus eye is a wonder of the underwater kingdom. An octopus's pupil is a horizontal stripe, rather than a round dot like a human eye, but in other ways our eyes are similar. Both human

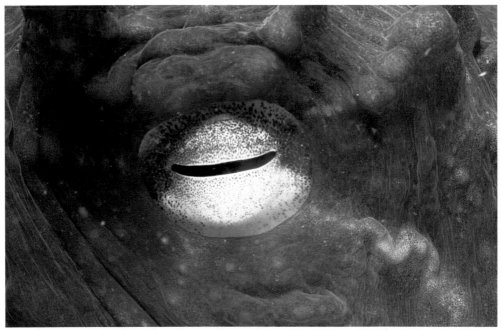

The octopus views the world through a horizontal pupil instead of a round one like humans have.

eyes and octopus eyes have many of the same structures: pupils, eyelids, irises, crystalline lenses, and retinas. Although most researchers believe that octopuses cannot see colors, their ability to perceive texture and tone makes their eyesight at least as good as that of fishes. The elastic octopus can turn its eyes 180°, allowing it to look behind itself without turning its head. It is as if it literally had eyes in the back of its head.

Octopuses are shy and solitary. When they aren't out hunting for food, they live alone inside a den under a ledge, in a pile of

Both the octopus and this moon snail belong to the phylum Mollusca.

rubble, or inside a coral cave. If there are no dens available, they may build their own from rocks, broken glass, or even discarded bottles. Octopuses aren't interested in other octopuses, except briefly during mating season. At any other time, if a larger octopus happens upon a smaller octopus, it might well eat it. The octopus also eats other members of its extended family, the mollusks. Clams, scallops, oysters, and snails, as well as squids and octopuses, are all mollusks, or "soft-bodied" animals.

A Head Above the Rest

Octopuses, squids, cuttlefishes, and chambered nautiluses make up a special group of mollusks—the *cephalopods*—that evolved almost 500 million years ago. Cephalopod means "head-footed" animal, named for the way the appendages grow directly out from the head. Cephalopods have arms encircling a mouth and a hard beak, and most species have suckers on the arms with which to capture food. The rest of the animal is made up of a muscular sac or mantle (commonly referred to as the head), which contains the hearts (three of them), kidneys, brain, and other organs. Gills extract oxygen from the water. After water passes over the gills, it is released through a funnel or siphon. When water is expelled forcefully out of the funnel by contraction of muscles of the mantle, it jet propels the creature through the water.

As in humans, the blood carries oxygen throughout the body to organs and muscles to fuel their work. But the octopus's copper-based blue blood is not as efficient an oxygen carrier as our own

*This octopus makes it clear why it is called
a cephalopod—a "head-footed" animal.*

Diagram of an octopus

red, iron-based blood. Because of this, a fleeing octopus quickly runs out of energy, like an out-of-shape jogger.

Except for the giant Pacific octopus, most octopuses are small, usually no larger than one to two feet long. Many species are just a few inches long. They live in nearly every ocean of the world, although more varieties live in warm waters. Some species are found right next to the shoreline, while others live in permanent darkness thousands of feet below the ocean surface. Most live brief lives, about one to two years. Even the giant Pacific octopus only lives about three years.

A frightened giant Pacific octopus squirts a cloud of ink to distract its pursuer.

Chapter Three

Who Needs a Shell?

The earliest ancestors of cephalopods were mollusks with thick shells that protected them from the predators that were evolving ever larger in the ancient seas. Of the estimated 1,000 species of cephalopods alive today, only the chambered nautilus still has a hard outer shell, although the cuttlefish and squid have remnants of an internal shell.

Our modern octopus has come a long way from its ancestors.

Although it has lost its protective shell, it has evolved amazing defensive strategies that more than compensate—a flexible body, agility, surprising intelligence, and the ability to camouflage itself with ink and color. It has been called the chameleon of the sea, but the octopus can change its color far faster than any chameleon on land.

Jacques Cousteau once described the octopus as "a creature designed for flight." That is just what a frightened octopus tries to do. The classic octopus defense is to squirt a cloud of ink, turn white, and jet propel to safety. It then changes its body color and skin texture to disappear against its background, or it may squeeze its supple body into a secret hiding place. No wonder the octopus has been called "the phantom of the sea."

If surprised by an enemy, the octopus squirts out a cloud of dark ink and mucous, which hangs in the water for several seconds. The inkblot, roughly the shape and size of the octopus, draws the attention of the attacker while the octopus changes color and escapes. Scientists think the ink may even temporarily numb the predator's sense of smell. If an octopus is vigorously pursued, it may ink half a dozen times in less than a minute.

When an octopus is attacked by an enemy such as a moray eel, the scene is a blur of writhing arms and snapping jaws. The octopus may lose an arm in the fight. The severed arm may twitch for several minutes. While the predator turns its attack on the wriggling arm, the wounded octopus pales and darts away. It will soon grow back its lost limb.

If the octopus can't escape, camouflage may protect it. Its skin becomes smooth or pebbly, depending on the texture of the rock or coral background. It takes on the color of its hiding place. For

Octopus is a favorite meal of moray eels. An octopus may lose an arm during a struggle with a moray, but the lost limb will grow back.

an animal that can't see colors, the octopus has a surprisingly acute color sense. Tiny sacs of pigment in the skin lighten or darken to create a range of shades and patterns to mimic its backdrop. *Chromatophores*, the color cells in its skin, can contract into small dots which make the octopus appear lighter. When the color cells expand, they create a darker color.

This small New England octopus changes color in the blink of an eye, thanks to color cells called chromatophores. *(See photo opposite.)*

Even baby octopuses in their eggs can change color. The common octopus, *Octopus vulgaris*, an octopus widely distributed throughout the world's oceans, hatches with 65 to 80 chromatophores. This number will increase to one to two million chromatophores by the time it reaches adulthood.

Color changes in the octopus are not only for defense; they also reveal its mood. A frightened octopus may turn white. An angry or excited octopus might blush a deep red. The pattern of a contented octopus might be a patchwork of gray, white, and brown. During mating, a dizzying display of stripes and colors probably reflects intense emotion.

Wily Hunters

When hunting, the octopus glides ghostlike over the ocean floor, extending its leading arms and then pulling its rear arms up behind. At times it seems to hover just above the ocean floor. At other times it strolls across the ocean bottom in long, rapid strides.

An octopus also moves by jet propulsion. It takes water into its mantle through an opening near the front of its bulbous body. Then, with a strong contraction of its muscles, it forces the water out through the funnel. The octopus rockets backwards, like a balloon suddenly releasing its air.

An octopus pumps water in through its mantle opening and out through its funnel to help it breathe and move.

The sensitive suckers of an octopus can feel and taste, and they can also exert a powerful grip.

Each of its eight arms may have up to 240 highly sensitive suction cups lined up in double rows, for a total of nearly 2,000 suckers. Three opposing sets of muscles in each sucker disc allow it to bend, contract, or stretch at any point. A sucker grips an object, whether it's a crab, a rock, or a human hand, by lowering the pressure inside the sucker to create a vacuum seal—much like the lid on a jar of homemade jam. The octopus can fold its suckers over objects as small as a pebble or as slender as a fishing line.

An octopus finds prey by poking its arms into cracks and crevices. The suckers not only grab prey, they taste it as well. The rims of these suckers are loaded with sensory organs called *chemoreceptors* that can smell and taste. The suckers can even distinguish a live clam from a dead one. As with our own fingers, the skin of the suckers is shed frequently to keep them sensitive and agile.

An octopus depends on its exceptional senses of vision and smell to track its prey. When an octopus spies a crab on the ocean floor, it opens up its web—the fold of skin between each arm— creating a pouch. It closes around the prey like an umbrella and carries its dinner back to its den inside a sac of water. The octopus secretes a chemical into this water-filled pouch that tranquilizes combative crabs and other prey.

Marine biologist Jim Cosgrove has observed the effects of this drug. "If we catch an octopus that's been hunting and shake out the crabs, they fall to the bottom and sit there absolutely dopey for 10 or 15 seconds. Then, as the crabs stagger away, the water suddenly hits their gills, and they snap to and run off."

Back in the safety of its den, the octopus may rip apart the shell of the crab, using its flexible suckers. Or it may crack open the shell with a parrotlike beak hidden inside the mouth, which is at the center of it arms. Its bite releases a poison that paralyzes or kills its prey.

For thick-shelled prey like clams or cockles, the octopus drills a hole through the shell with its *radula*, a filelike tongue covered with small, sharp teeth. It injects powerful enzymes that soften the meat into a thick liquid, an octopus "milk shake." The octopus then sucks its meal out through the hole. After picking its prey clean, the tidy octopus tosses the empty shell out the door.

By opening the web between each arm, the octopus drifts down through the water like a parachute.

Not Just Nocturnal

Many popular books about cephalopods claim that octopuses hunt only at night, but a research study in British Columbia proved just how outgoing octopuses can be. Jim Cosgrove and Dr. Jennifer Mather of the University of Lethbridge in Alberta, Canada, discovered that giant Pacific octopuses don't hide in their dens all day as people had assumed. In a three-week-long experiment, the researchers put radio tags on several octopuses, so they could track their movements 24 hours a day. The scientists had expected to sleep during the day and monitor the octopuses' travels by radio at night. Instead, the small research team had to set up three eight-hour shifts because their subjects went out *all* the time! The octopuses spent as much time away from their dens hunting during the day as they did at night. Each trip lasted about 50 minutes. At night, the octopuses just explored farther from their dens. By the end of three sleepless weeks, Jim recalls, "We were all exhausted and getting a little testy on that boat."

Are Octopuses Dangerous?

Despite the tales of Victor Hugo and Jules Verne, humans are never the intended victims of octopuses, even of the large Pacific octopus. However, a diver who pokes his hand into an octopus den may find that several strong arms prevent him from pulling it out again. The octopus may have mistaken the hand for prey, or it may simply be trying to defend itself from an intruder. If the diver doesn't panic under the grip, the octopus will usually tire

28

A giant octopus eats a fish it has captured. Scientists have learned that octopuses may hunt both during the day and at night.

quickly and release its hold with the diver unharmed. A diving expert, Max Gene Nohl, once wrote, "The chance of a diver being attacked by an octopus is as remote as the possibility of a hunter in the woods being attacked by a rabbit."

The only truly dangerous octopus is one of the smallest. The four-inch-long blue-ringed octopus of the South Pacific has a venomous bite that can kill a human in just a few minutes. The blue-ringed octopus often scours tidepools along the shore for mol-

The blue-ringed octopus is beautiful but deadly. Its venomous bite can kill a human within minutes.

lusks, crabs, and shrimp. A curious beachcomber who picks up the cute creature will never do it again. The octopus's blue rings darken in alarm. Then the tiny octopus nips its attacker, injecting a powerful toxin into the wound. The poison, called *tetrodoxin*, is not produced by the octopus itself, but by several different kinds of bacteria living within its body. This poison is even found in the octopus's tentacles, ink sac, and eggs, suggesting that it may be used for defense as well as for killing prey. Some scientists claim that the venom of female blue-ringed octopuses becomes more powerful when they are protecting their eggs.

Millions of octopuses are harvested each year and sold in fish markets like this one in Tokyo, Japan.

31

Instead of asking if octopuses are dangerous to humans, a more appropriate question might be: Are humans dangerous to octopuses? Mediterranean fishermen have been catching octopuses for thousands of years by lowering clay pots into the water on the end of a line. When an octopus crawls into this new shelter on the ocean floor, the fisherman reels in the pot with the octopus huddled in the bottom. In some places, populations of octopuses have been overfished almost to the point of extinction. Although giant octopuses are also hunted for food, this population of octopuses may suffer more from human activities like pulp and paper processing that may add chemicals to seawater or remove vital oxygen from it.

Chapter Four

Brainy Cephalopod

The octopus's brain is huge compared to the animal's overall size, which is not surprising for a creature that is basically a head with arms. Without the safety of a shell, the octopus has had to develop an ability to recognize and react to danger instantly. No other invertebrate can match its intelligence.

Octopus Learning

Octopus researchers have done all sorts of tests on octopuses to try to gauge how smart they are. Laboratory octopuses have learned how to run mazes, solve puzzles, recognize objects by touch, and sometimes outsmart the scientists. One octopus used to sneak out of its aquarium tank each night, crawl into nearby tanks to eat fish, and then return to its own tank before the researchers arrived back at work the next morning!

In one experiment, an octopus was given a lobster, a favorite treat. The lobster, however, was inside a glass jar secured by a cork lid. The octopus could see the lobster through the glass and barely touch it with one arm through a hole in the cork. After

In laboratory experiments, octopuses have been able to figure out how to open a sealed jar in order to reach a prize like this spiny lobster.

several attempts to engulf the lobster and the jar, the octopus realized it would have to remove the lid to get at its prey. Moments later, out popped the cork. The next time that the octopus was given the same problem, it solved it in much less time, showing that the octopus had learned from experience.

In another experiment, researchers would offer an octopus a crab, sometimes placing it into the tank along with a white plastic disk. Whenever the octopus reached for the crab when the disk was present, the octopus would receive a mild electric shock. The octopus soon learned not to go near the crab if the white disk was there, too. Even two to three weeks later, the octopus would react the same way to the warning of the white disk. It remembered what it had learned.

Learning by watching requires an intelligence usually reserved for advanced forms of life like dolphins and humans. But two Italian researchers discovered that "What octopuses see, octopuses do." Their octopuses learned to perform a simple task simply by watching another octopus do it first. The researchers placed two balls—one red, one white—inside the tanks of their subjects. By rewarding them when they chose the white ball and punishing them when they chose the red ball, the scientists trained one group of octopuses to always choose the white ball. Another group was trained to select the red ball.

Once the octopuses were trained, they performed the trick for untrained octopuses watching from an adjoining tank. Each spectator watched the demonstration four times. Then they were tested to see if they could perform the trick. The watchers not only chose the right ball, they learned to do it faster, and with fewer mistakes, than the octopuses the scientists had trained. The researchers hadn't expected octopuses, who live alone in nature, to be such good observers. Since their mothers die as soon as the eggs hatch, octopuses aren't able to learn by watching their mothers as many baby animals do. Perhaps young octopuses learn the skills they need to survive by observing other, larger octopuses without themselves being seen (or else they might get eaten!). More experiments in octopus intelligence will determine if they are really as brainy as this experiment suggests.

Can Humans and Octopuses Be Friends?

In captivity, octopuses seem to be able to recognize their caretakers. They will often rise to the surface when their aquarist appears. Besides feeding and caring for the octopus's health, an aquarist has to make the animal feel secure by providing a place where it can hide.

Aquarist Mike Callahan of the New England Aquarium in Massachusetts has built a secluded shelter inside the tank for his giant octopus. He feeds it two or three squid each day, and an occasional treat of shrimp, fish, or crab. (He thoughtfully removes the crab's claws first, so they won't pinch the octopus.) Oftentimes, when Mike opens the lid of the tank to feed it, the giant octopus pulls itself up and hangs over the side of the tank, feeling everything within its reach, including Mike. The octopus even allows itself to be scratched. It wraps its arms around its keeper's arm (although it doesn't seem to like to touch his clothing). When Mike pulls the suckers off his arm, it produces a sound like champagne bottles popping their corks.

Some octopuses can be downright mischievous. One octopus

at the Waikiki Aquarium used to grab the hand of its feeder and try to push it into the spines of a poisonous sea urchin with which it shared the tank. Another octopus used to squirt a stream of water at one particular aquarist every time she passed its tank.

Devotion and Death

Another characteristic that separates octopuses from most other spineless sea creatures is their devotion to their young. Parenthood is a responsibility that octopuses take very seriously—to the point of death.

Octopus courtship is not a long, drawn-out affair, although mating can be. In giant octopuses, the largest male in the neighborhood is usually the first in line outside the den of a female that is ready to mate. Jim Cosgrove in British Columbia has observed that "A large male will stand just outside a female's den, and a smaller male will wait five to six feet away, and still smaller males another six-foot distance away."

When an octopus mates, the male passes sperm packets called *spermatophores* down a groove in his third right arm. A special spoon-shaped tip, called the *hectocotylus*, scoops the spermatophores into the female's mantle opening. Octopuses often mate for several hours. (Researcher Jim Cosgrove hasn't been able to stay underwater long enough to find out if the female mates with one or more males.)

After mating, the female returns to her den. She may build a wall of stones to seal the entrance to her cave. She attaches strings of eggs to the ceiling of the den until up to 50,000 or more eggs hang like glass beads from the roof of the cave. She squirts water

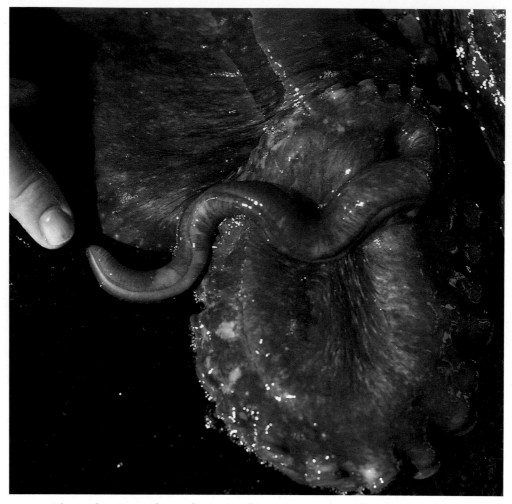

The male octopus has a hectocotylus, *a spoon-shaped tip at the end of one arm to transfer sperm packets to the female.*

over them with her funnel to keep the eggs clean and to supply oxygen to the developing babies.

She won't leave the den to hunt and even refuses handouts of food that a diver might offer her. She loses more than half her body weight and eventually starves to death. If she dies before the

Giant octopus eggs hatching. Octopus eggs hang from the roof of the female's den.

39

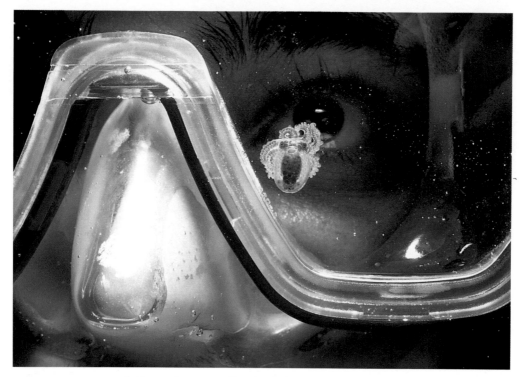
A tiny octopus confronts a strange new creature.

eggs hatch, they will probably perish, too. Crabs, sea stars, and small fishes will invade the nest and eat the mother and the unhatched eggs.

Hatching time varies with water temperature. In the cold waters of the North Pacific Ocean, it may take six and one-half months for giant octopus eggs to hatch. The eggs of tropical octopuses usually hatch in less than six weeks. When they emerge, the baby octopuses look like miniature adults. Tiny octopuses the size of a pinkie fingernail can already change color, squirt ink, and jet propel backwards.

Although the eggs usually hatch at night, predators are quick to discover the newborn octopuses. Most of the hatchlings will be devoured by hungry fishes within their first half hour of freedom. Only a very few offspring will grow up to reproduce themselves. Luckily for the little octopuses, those that do survive grow amazingly fast.

About the only time you might see two octopuses together is during mating or hatching. Since you will hardly ever encounter more than one octopus at a time, perhaps you haven't given much thought to the proper way to refer to more than one octopus. You may call them octopus, octopi, or octopuses, or you could address them as octopods, polypuses, or octopussycats. Call them what you will, octopuses are shy creatures that are most content when left alone.

The squid has ten appendages: eight arms plus two feeding tentacles. Its tentacles
are kept hidden until they shoot out to seize prey.

Chapter Five

Cephalopod Society

$\mathbf{B}$esides the octopus, the cephalopod class of mollusks includes the squid, the cuttlefish, and the chambered nautilus. Each one has is own peculiar characteristics.

The Squid

Squids are the sprinters of the sea. They jet propel backwards so rapidly that few predators and no diver can match their speed.

The adults of some species can even reach 25 mph! Squids can also flutter along by slowly rippling slender fins that run along the sides of the body.

Squids are aggressive hunters equipped with two long feeding tentacles in addition to eight shorter arms. Their suckers are lined with teeth for grasping prey. Squids range in size from about one inch to the giant squid that may be 60 feet long, including the tentacles.

Some squids hunt in packs. When they mate, they also gather in large congregations. Thousands of squids mate and lay clusters of pale, torpedo-shaped eggs. Then they die. Many animals, including whales, sharks, cod, and seals, gather at the mating grounds to feed on the squid, living and dead.

Squids, like octopuses, can change color. Many are also *bioluminescent*—they can light up. Bacteria living under the skin of some squid produce tiny glittering lights. Deep-water squid, which live thousands of feet below the surface, create their own light. Light-producing organs called *photophores* make two chemicals: a protein called *lucerferin* and an enzyme called *luciferase*. When the two mix together, the enzyme chemically breaks down the protein, releasing a pale, blue-green light. This is the same process fireflies use to make their rear ends blink on and off.

Squids may use light to lure prey, confuse predators, or to communicate with other squids. Some species squirt clouds of glowing bacteria instead of ink. While the predator is absorbed in the light show, the squid escapes.

Squids, like humans, have nervous systems. Some squids have nerve cells about a hundred times bigger than human nerve cells, which makes them much easier to study. Squid *axons* that connect

Many squid are bioluminescent—they can light up.

the brain to nerve cells to muscles may be as large as the diameter of pencil lead. Researchers at Woods Hole Marine Biological Laboratory in Massachusetts study the squid's nervous system in order to try to learn how malfunctions in the human nervous system contribute to Alzheimer's, Parkinson's, and Lou Gehrig's diseases. Other scientists are stretching squid axons to see how much strain a nerve can take before it is damaged. What they learn may someday help prevent sports injuries on the playing field.

Japanese researchers believe that squids may also serve as excellent indicators of ocean pollution. Squid livers concentrate high levels of pollutants like PCBs. Because a squid lives only a year on the average, its liver can gauge the accumulation of ocean pollution over that year. By comparing different years of squid, we

45

*Squid as food is a highly prized delicacy in many countries,
but the United States is not one of them.*

may be able to gain a sense of how the level of pollution in the
sea is changing.

Squids are highly prized as food by many peoples. There are
extensive fisheries in Spain, Portugal, and Japan. Some people
would be hard pressed to think of any better use for squid than
as Japanese *sushi* or Italian *calamari*. In the United States, most
squid are exported or sold as bait.

Everything about the giant squid (*Architeuthis*) is huge, from
its eyes to its beak to its long tentacles. A giant squid's eyes, the
size of automobile headlights, search the gloom of the deep sea
for prey. It may measure up to 60 feet long (from the tip of its
body to outstretched feeding tentacles). Some giant squids have
been known to weigh 1,000 pounds. Each ring of suckers is sur-
rounded by small, sharp teeth that dig into the flesh of its prey.

The beak of a giant squid has been known to bite through steel cable.

Giant squids live, scientists guess, anywhere from about 1,000 feet to perhaps 3,000 feet down in the sea. Scientists aren't sure just how deep giant squids live because no human has ever seen them in their natural habitat. Occasionally, people encounter dead or dying giant squids washed ashore, tangled in fishing nets, or floating at the surface of the sea.

Giant squids are the major diet of sperm whales, which dive deep into the sea in search of them. Although the battle-scarred whales often show the imprint of suckers on their skin, dozens of squid beaks inside their stomachs show that the whales are the ultimate winners.

Jules Verne's submarine, *The Nautilus*, wrestled with a giant squid in his story *Twenty Thousand Leagues Under the Sea*, but has there ever been a documented case of a giant squid killing or injuring a person? Many people say no, despite the fact that on July 4, 1874, *The London Times* reported that the schooner *Pearl* and its crew were sunk by a giant squid in the Bay of Bengal, after the captain shot at it with a rifle.

The Cuttlefish

The cuttlefish can swim by jet propulsion like the squid and, like the octopus, can eject a dark-colored cloud of ink to confuse enemies. But its most remarkable characteristic is its ability to change color, which scientists believe is one way it communicates with other cuttlefishes. A cuttlefish may exhibit thirty different color patterns that include light and dark coloration, fake eye-

Cuttlefish can change color rapidly and create a variety of different patterns.

spots, zebra stripes, and dice patterns. Their dizzying color changes help them blend in with their background, startle predators, attract a mate, and conquer rivals during courtship.

Two of the cuttlefish's ten appendages are longer than the rest. Most of the time, they stay tucked up under the other arms. But if prey ventures within range, these tentacles shoot out to grab an unsuspecting shrimp or fish and drag it to the cuttlefish's sharp beak.

Next to octopuses, cuttlefishes are probably the most intelligent invertebrates. In the laboratory, cuttlefishes can learn to recognize which colored discs signal food and which don't. Their intelligence reveals itself at an early age. The minute a baby cuttlefish hatches, it knows how and when to bury itself in the sand, squirt ink, change color, and retreat as larger animals approach. It instantly recognizes small prey and orients its body to be able to grab passing shrimp with its darting tentacles. With practice, it learns how to hunt efficiently for larger prey, like crabs. After being pinched a few times, a young cuttlefish figures out that it is best to sneak up on a crab from behind.

Although most people would be surprised to see a cuttlefish in a pet store, part of it, at least, is quite common there. The cuttlebone, the cuttlefish's internal shell of horny material buried within the mantle, is sold as a source of calcium for parakeets and other pet birds. Tiny chambers within the cuttlebone hold gases that allow the cuttlefish to hover weightless above the ocean floor. The cuttlefish can pump liquid into the cuttlebone to become less buoyant and sink to the bottom.

This cuttlefish seems to be right on top of the diver's mask.

Another useful part of the cuttlefish is its ink, which was the original *India ink*, a dark pigment also called *sepia*. It was used in quill pens in Colonial days and is still used today by artists for drawing and lettering. The ink is also valued for a mysterious ingredient that Japanese researchers are testing as a possible cure for cancer.

The Chambered Nautilus

Meet a living fossil. The chambered nautilus resembles its ancient extinct ancestors, the nautiloids, more than it does any of its living relatives, the octopus, squid, or cuttlefish. Five hundred million years ago, the nautiloids were the masters of the sea. Then there were over 2,500 species, some with straight shells, others with the coiled shell of the modern nautilus.

Now only six species of nautiluses remain, submerged deep in the Indian and South Pacific oceans. They live from about 60 feet to 1,500 feet, usually along reef walls that plunge to the depths of the ocean. On moonless nights, they migrate closer to the surface to feed on the molted shells of spiny lobsters, on small fishes, and shrimp.

Nautiluses cannot change color or squirt ink like other cephalopods, but they do have an external shell that no other cephalopods possess. They have 80 to 100 arms that surround the head in two rows. Each arm can touch and taste, but does not have suckers to hold onto prey.

The nautilus gets its name from the many walled chambers—partitioned "rooms"—inside its shell. An adult nautilus may have 30 to 38 chambers. The animal lives in the outermost chamber

Photograph by Paul Humann

*The chambered nautilus is the only cephalopod to retain a hard outer shell
like its ancient ancestors. It is called a "living fossil."*

and uses the others to regulate its buoyancy. By adjusting the
amount of gas (mostly nitrogen) and liquid (similar to seawater)
in the chambers, it can move up or down fairly rapidly.

The beauty of its shell has also been the curse of the chambered nautilus. Some nautilus fisherman say that over 5,000 living
animals are taken each year in the Philippines alone to supply
shell dealers. This estimate is probably very low, as they are col-
lected extensively in India and Indonesia, too.

The nautilus lives longer than any other cephalopod. Nautilus eggs, cemented to rocks or coral on the seafloor, take a year to hatch. When a baby nautilus emerges from its egg case, it is already an inch across. It may grow up to reproduce 15 to 20 years later. Unlike the octopus that mates and then dies, the chambered nautilus lives on after reproduction.

Glossary

aquarist A person who cares for aquarium animals; a curator.

axon The part of a nerve cell through which impulses travel.

bacteria Microscopic one-celled organisms, some of which are beneficial while others cause diseases.

bioluminescence A light produced in certain animals by a chemical reaction or by bacteria.

buoyancy The degree to which an object is able to float in or on water.

cephalopod The most advanced group of mollusks, characterized by head, arms, and hard beak.

chemoreceptor Sensory organ on the rim of an octopus sucker that perceives taste and smell.

chromatophore Specialized skin cell that contracts or expands to change the color of an animal.

dry suit A dive suit that prevents water from getting next to the skin.

enzyme A substance in a plant or animal that acts as a catalyst to speed up or cause a chemical reaction.

funnel A tubelike structure in cephalopods used in locomotion and in breathing; also called a siphon.

hectocotylus The tip of one arm of the male octopus shaped like a spoon in order to scoop sperm packets into the female's mantle opening.

invertebrate Animal without a backbone. Ninety-five percent of all the animals in the sea are invertebrates.

kraken A legendary sea monster of tremendous size.

lucerferase An enzyme that acts with lucerferin to produce light.

lucerferin A substance that produces light by combining with oxygen in the presence of lucerferase.

mantle Also called the "head" and encloses the gills and internal organs of the octopus.

mollusk Second largest group of invertebrates, characterized by a soft, unsegmented body consisting of a head or mantle and muscular foot (or feet); with or without a shell.

photophore A light-producing organ.

PCBs Polychlorobiphenyls, a group of chemicals that resist breaking down in the environment and so may build up to dangerous levels of poisonous pollutants.

radula A mollusk's filelike tongue covered with small, sharp teeth.

spermatophore A small packet of sperm that the male transfers into the female during mating.

tetrodoxin A powerful poison that attacks the nerves, causing symptoms that may include cramps, muscle pain, paralysis, and death.

toxin Poison.

web The fold of skin between each arm of an octopus.

Bibliography

Conklin, Gladys. *The Octopus and Other Cephalopods*. Holiday House, New York, 1977.

Cousteau, Jacques-Yves and Philippe Diole. *Octopus and Squid: The Soft Intelligence*. Doubleday and Co., New York, 1973.

Lauber, Patricia. *An Octopus Is Amazing*. HarperCollins Children's Books, New York, 1990.

Martin, James. *Tentacles: The Amazing World of Octopus, Squid, and Their Relatives*. Crown Publishers, New York, 1993.

"Eye to Eye with the Giant Octopus." *National Geographic*, March, 1992, pp. 86–97.

Index